A Little Book of
Bobcats

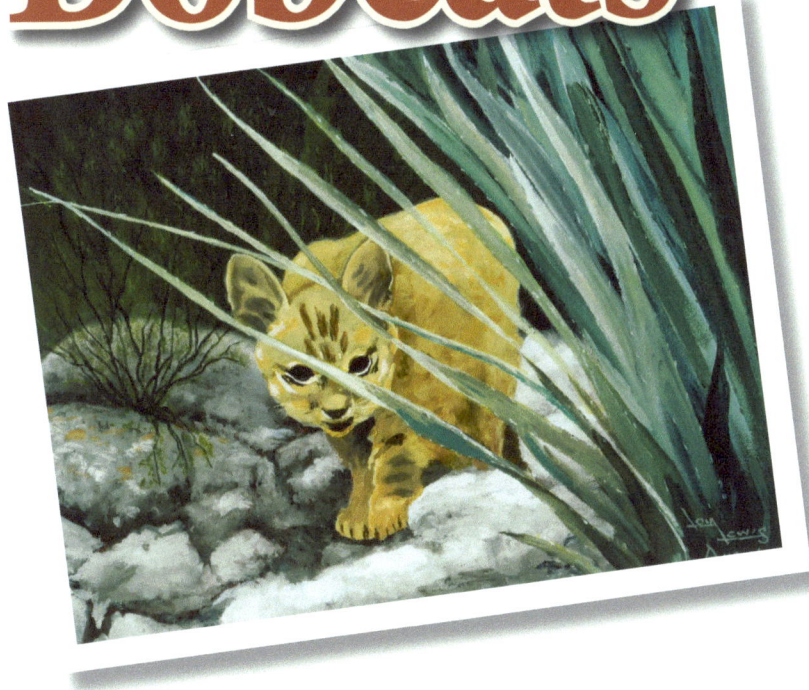

By Diane R. Hanover

Illustrations by Lou Lewis

Picture Rocks Publications
Tucson, Arizona
www.picturerockspublications.com

Illustrations by Lou Lewis: p. 1 *The Lookout;* p. 3 *Three of a Kind;* p. 4 *At Attention;* p. 7 *Always Alert;*
p. 11 *Still a Little Shaky;* p. 12 *Everybody's Welcome;* p. 17 *Snow on the Catalinas;* p. 18 *A Whole New World;*
p. 21 *See You Later;* p. 23 *Leave Some for Me;* p. 25 *Will It Bite?;* p. 26 *Sunrise on the Catalinas.*

Photo credits Rhonda Spencer rdavs@msn.com: pp. 2, 6, 9 *top,* 15, 27, 30
Photo credits Merry S. Lewis: pp. 9 *bottom,* 19, 20, 32 *bottom*

ISBN 978-0-9968419-6-2

Text copyright ©2015 Diane R. Hanover
Illustrations and photographs copyright ©2015 Merry S. Lewis
Photographs copyright ©2015 Rhonda Spencer

A Little Book of Bobcats / Diane R. Hanover; illustrations by Lou Lewis.

Summary: Bobcats, the most common wild feline in North America, are normally elusive creatures, but in the
foothills of Tucson, Arizona, they dwell untroubled among humans.—Provided by publisher.

Book design by Cynthia Hannon
CynthiaHannon.com

For Lou Lewis,
whose love of his backyard bobcats is evident
in every brushstroke.

Most people have never seen a wild bobcat. Masters of concealment, they use many types of cover to stay out of sight.

Bobcats are the most common wild cat in North America—but few people have ever seen one. With their spotted and striped fur, these felines are masters of camouflage. They hide in shadowy brush or among rock piles and ledges. They crouch with focused patience, waiting for a rabbit or a rat to hop by. When game is scarce, they search their home ranges in a zigzag pattern. Keeping mostly under cover, they look and listen for quarry. Hunting at dawn and dusk or whenever their prey is about, bobcats live solitary lives. And they typically keep their distance from humans.

Except, that is, in a few special places. In the desert foothills near the city of Tucson, Arizona, bobcats and people have come to share a kind of neutral zone. Instead of avoiding the presence of humans, some bobcats live among them in plain view. Why this is so isn't fully understood. Biologists who study the matter are both puzzled and charmed, as are many of the homeowners who dwell in peace with these feisty predators.

Bobcats in the foothills of Tucson may live
and raise kittens in a desert backyard.

3

Unlike most bobcats living in desert lands,
Tucson wildcats often have red-colored fur.

4

Bobcats Are Wildcats

The bobcats of Tucson have much in common with bobcats in other regions. They all share the same scientific name: *Lynx rufus*, which means "red lynx" in Latin. Bobcats in northern, forested habitats tend to have rusty or red-brown fur. In more arid habitats, pelage (fur) may be gray-brown. However, in the Sonoran Desert near Tucson, bobcats often sport reddish fur.

Bobcats or bobtailed cats come by their common name because of their short, bobbed tails. Typically, males have tails about six inches long. Females' tails average about five inches. (By comparison, the average male house cat has an 11-inch tail. A female has an almost 10-inch tail.) However, a running bobcat bobs or dips up and down at full speed. That may be a source of its common name as well.

In many parts of the country, bobcats are known as wildcats. Many high schools and colleges have named their team mascots the wildcats, including the University of Arizona.

The Features of a Bobcat

Along with colorful red- or gray-brown fur, bobcats show beautiful random patterns of dark spots and stripes on their backs, and on their white inner legs and bellies. A dark streak of fur may run along a bobcat's spine, like a jaunty blaze down its back. The tail has stripes on top and underside fur of white. Markings on bobcat fur may be faint or quite distinct, depending on the animal. A bobcat's spotted and striped coat enables it to hide among the shadows, blending with its environment.

A bobcat's powerful hind legs make it a graceful jumper.

Apart from its bobbed tail, a bobcat has three other distinctive features: a facial ruff, tufted ears, and long legs. A facial ruff is a collar of fur around an animal's face. On bobcats, it looks something like a beard or long sideburns. The fur ruff may be striped with black and quite eye-catching.

Bobcats' large ears are also distinctive. At the tips, tufts of black hair point stiffly upward. Some researchers think the small spears of hair may enhance the animals' hearing. White splotches mark the backs of bobcat ears.

A bobcat's long muscular legs provide a lengthened stride for running. The hind legs, which are powerful and longer than the front legs, are designed for jumping.

Bobcats are medium-sized felines. They can grow to about twice the size of domestic cats. Typically, they range in weight from 15 to 35 pounds. Weight depends on the age of an animal and the availability of food. The average male is 22 pounds. The average female is 16 pounds. Bobcats stand 18 to 24 inches tall at the shoulder. They may reach 24 to 48 inches long. The felines that live farther north tend to be larger than those in the south.

Comparing Bobcats and Mountain Lions

Despite their smaller size, bobcats are often mistaken for mountain lions. In southern Arizona, most reported sightings of mountain lions turn out to be bobcats. But it's actually easy to tell the difference. Mountain lions have a long tail, up to a yard in length. Compare that to the five to six inch tail of a bobcat!

Mountain lions can weigh between 70 and 150 pounds. That's as much as four times more than a large bobcat!

Mountain lions tend to be one color—tawny—all over. Bobcats have a variety of colors, including black and white, spots, and stripes.

To identify a mountain lion, look for a large wild feline with a long tail, much bigger than a bobcat. Lion fur is mostly one color—tan or light brown.

To identify a bobcat, look for a colorful, mid-sized cat with a short tail, long legs, tufted ears, and a facial ruff.

9

How Bobcats Hunt

Bobcats are skilled and solitary predators. That means that lone bobcats hunt and kill other animals for food. Rather than chasing down prey, bobcats hunt using two other tactics: search and ambush. They may use stealth to hunt through their home range until they chance upon something to eat. Or they may hide and wait for dinner to come to them. Sometimes they combine search and ambush.

Traveling the home range for food, a bobcat zigzags through its territory. It skirts the open, using the cover of trees, brush, cactus, and outcroppings to cloak its movements. Silent as grass, the hunter moves on padded feet. At game trails, it stops to listen, waiting patiently for a cottontail or pack rat to appear. There! A jackrabbit hops into view. Spotting its prey, the wildcat crouches noiselessly. It creeps forward under cover, careful to remain unseen. When the target is within the strike zone (33 feet or less), the cat pounces. With lightning speed and razor claws, it traps the jackrabbit and dispatches it with a quick bite of sharp fangs.

Of course, the prey may get away. And bobcats, which are powerfully built for short bursts of speed, might give up after a chase of only ten feet.

Bobcat kittens learn early to stalk prey in stealth.

What Bobcats Eat

Opportunistic hunters. That's what wildcats are. It means they'll eat anything they can catch! But they are also obligate carnivores. That means they only eat meat, except that they may sometimes eat grass. They also rarely scavenge, or look for food discarded by others, as do predators such as coyotes. When it comes to food, bobcats prefer to hunt for themselves.

In southern Arizona, bobcats' favorite meal is lagomorphs—cottontail rabbits and jackrabbits—and rodents, such as mice and pack rats. About 65 percent of their diet comes from lagomorphs and rodents. But bobcats eat an array of small prey, including lizards, snakes, quail, and other birds. If they can, they'll even take down larger animals such as deer, pronghorn and bighorn sheep, and javelina. In fact, a typical bobcat can drop an animal eight times its own weight.

When humans settle in bobcat habitat, animals of value to people sometimes become prey. Bobcats may plunder farms for livestock, such as rabbits, chickens, sheep, and goats. They may also prey on domestic cats and dogs.

Cottontails and their jackrabbit cousins are lagomorphs, mammals that include rabbits and hares. They are among bobcats' favorite foods.

However, bobcats provide a valuable service to humans. In the Sonoran Desert, they help to control rodent and lagomorphs populations. Rodents and rabbits normally reproduce at tremendously fast rates. Without bobcats to prey on them, their populations could easily unbalance the desert ecosystem. Bobcats living on the fringes of urban areas also prey on mice, Norway rats, and pack rats—rodents that tend to be unpopular with their human hosts.

Hunters as Prey

Fierce predators, bobcats rely on a variety of skills to survive. Yet they are often in danger themselves. In the wild, adult bobcats can live up to 13 years—but often don't. Studies suggest that to have high rates of survival, bobcats need plenty of available food and protection from people. In other words, they need a habitat with numerous rabbits and hares, and minimal interference from humans. Such factors increase survival rates, but don't remove major threats. Mountain lions, for instance, hunt adult bobcats for food. Many smaller predators, such as coyotes and raptors, prey on baby bobcats. Bobcats may become injured if their prey fights back or they brawl with other bobcats. When food is scarce, they may starve or succumb to disease. Humans, however, are often the number one cause of bobcat deaths.

Historically, humans have hunted, trapped, snared, and poisoned bobcats. These activities continue today. Bobcats may be seen as a threat to livestock. Or they may be prized for their attractive fur, which can be sold to the fashion industry for clothing and other uses. Or they simply may be captured and killed as game animals, tracked,

14

trapped, or treed with dogs. People may kill tens of thousands of bobcats in these ways each year.

One indirect human cause of bobcat deaths is loss of habitat. To survive, bobcats need a natural environment rich in sheltering cover and suitable prey. As human use of land expands—through the growth of cities and suburbs, as well as through new large-scale mining and logging operations—bobcat habitat shrinks. So do bobcat populations. Bobcats also die in accidents. Collisions with cars and trucks kill bobcats each year. Bobcats that climb power poles may be electrocuted.

Home Ranges

In 2010, researchers found that between two million and three and a half million bobcats roamed the United States. They believed that bobcat populations were increasing.

Today, bobcats appear to live everywhere in the United States, except Alaska, Hawaii, and possibly Delaware. They have adapted to a wide range of geographic conditions. Dense forests, high mountain ranges (although not the alpine zones above 12,000 feet), scrublands, and deserts all provide habitats in which bobcats feel at home. Wherever they live, the felines prefer areas with a variety of dense vegetation and cover for hunting, as well as high vantage points. Thick brush or rock cliffs and ledges offer shelter for rest and dens. Rivers, lakes, ponds, and springs provide water.

Bobcats roam in well-defined areas or home ranges. Solitary males may wander ranges as large as two square miles or more, while solitary females may use smaller plots. In fact, male home ranges may include two or three smaller female home ranges within their territory. The bobcats mark their home ranges with urine scent, claw scratches on trees, and scrapes on the ground. They know their rugged

Outside Tucson, Arizona, the Santa Catalina Mountains and their foothills provide home ranges for many bobcats.

home terrain well, and use it to hunt, rest, or rear young. Again and again, bobcats return to sites within their home ranges where they've slept or successfully hunted before. Over a period of weeks, they travel their territory. An abandoned shed, an old pack rat den, a rocky outcropping along a game trail, a pile of brush from a fallen tree—such sites may have yielded prey in past hunts and will do so again.

Family Life

When a female bobcat is a year old, she may mate with a male. Before her kittens are born, usually in spring, she chooses a den to shelter and protect them. Bobcat litters commonly hold two to four babies. A newborn kitten weighs just over five ounces—about the size of a small cell phone or a deck of cards.

The spotted fur of a bobcat kitten is soft and thick.

Like its mother, a bobcat kitten has white splotches on the back of its ears.

Born blind, the kittens may not open their eyes for up to 18 days. At first, they nurse most of the time. As they grow, their mother begins to leave the den to hunt for herself.

Bobcat kittens have soft, thick, spotted fur. They purr when content and mew when upset. Well-fed kittens grow quickly and explore their den. At about five weeks of age, they begin to leave the den to romp and play. Their mother teaches them to eat meat and to hunt by bringing prey, both live and dead, to the den. The kittens stalk small game, such as mice and birds, near their den. By the time they are three months old, they have begun following their mother on hunts. When they master hunting for themselves, they leave their mother and look for a home range of their own.

A bobcat kitten rests safely in a backyard.

Kittens learn hunting skills by following
and watching their mother.

Bobcats and Humans

Solitary, stealthy, and camouflaged, bobcats usually avoid humans. But they are well able to adapt to the challenge of human proximity. That's one reason they survive today in large numbers.

In Tucson, Arizona, many bobcats coexist with people in plain sight. The cactus-covered foothills of the Tucson and Catalina mountains provide habitat for the felines. Drainages and dry washes leading down from high places allow bobcats to travel easily through their home ranges. Though houses dot the desert hills, great swaths of prime habitat surround many homes and neighborhoods. Human-made elements may actually aid bobcat survival. Golf courses with ponds and grass attract cottontails and other prey. Yards with bushes and trees, fountains, walls, and other structures provide places for bobcats to rest, sun, drink, protect and raise kittens, and hunt.

Bobcat kittens drink from a backyard birdbath.

The bobcats of the Catalina foothills have found many friends. In some special cases, the wildcats may even trust them. In 2006, two Tucsonans discovered a bobcat family in their front yard. The three kittens, looking a lot like house cats, played in a culvert under the driveway. To the delight of the humans, the mother bobcat returned to give the kittens a lesson in how to climb a nearby palo verde tree. Scratch marks from baby bobcat claws can still be seen in that tree today.

A few days later, the mother bobcat surprised the people again. She jumped the six-foot wall surrounding their backyard, and brought her babies with her. Then she left them there while she went off to hunt! For hours the three kittens explored the enclosed yard. They rolled or slept in the grass, drank from the birdbath, and annoyed the two desert tortoises that lived in the backyard.

With some concern, the homeowners called the Arizona Game and Fish Department for advice. Said the official, That bobcat mother has probably been watching you for a while. She thinks her family will be safe in your yard. Just wait. She'll be back.

The official was right. The mother bobcat eventually came back for her kittens and took them with her. But they returned that summer, again and again. Each year since then, a mother bobcat and her kittens has visited that yard in spring and summer to sun, relax, sleep, and romp in safety.

Kittens examine a desert tortoise.

When did the bobcats of Tucson reach a parley with folks in the foothills? It's hard to tell. In other desert urban places, bobcats continue to avoid humans as much as possible. But a website for the local newspaper, *The Arizona Daily Star,* includes dozens of pictures of bobcats in the backyard, taken by friendly locals. The felines may hop a wall to drink from a birdbath, or loll in the sun on a warm adobe wall. They bring their kittens into the yards for fresh water, to sleep, or simply to play in a safe place.

Bobcats and You

To see a wild bobcat is a heart-pounding sight. Enjoy the view, but never approach one. These beautiful, wild predators should be treated with respect and left alone. Do not leave food out to feed them. It probably won't attract them but will bring other unwanted creatures, such as coyotes, skunks, and javelinas. Remember that bobcats prefer to hunt and catch prey. And prey includes house cats and small dogs. Make sure that your pets are secure out of doors. Provide fencing that includes a covered top. Or keep pets close by on a leash.

Always keep a safe distance from wildlife, including bobcats. In Arizona, there are no known attacks on people by a healthy bobcat. But rabies is not completely unknown in these populations, and if a bobcat displays strange behavior, report it.

Protecting bobcats and their habitat requires the attention of everyone. In Arizona, the Arizona Game and Fish Department provides helpful information on bobcats in their online "Living With Wildlife" series. You can search for "Living With Bobcats" to find it. There's also a Wild Cat Research and Conservation Center at the University of Arizona. The folks there work to conserve 36 species

of wild cats, including bobcats. They collaborate with biologists, students, and schools to inspire interest and understanding of wild cats around the world. Find them at **www.uawildcatresearch.org** and take part in studying and protecting these remarkable felines.

Glossary

alpine zone the region in high mountains above 10,800 feet in which trees do not grow.

biologist a scientist who studies living things, such as plants and animals.

camouflage the patterns or colors of an animal's fur that help it to hide.

environment the physical surroundings in which plants, animals, and people live.

feline of or relating to the cat family, Felidae, which includes bobcats, mountain lions, house cats, jaguars, tigers, lions, and so on.

foothills low hills at the base of a mountain range.

game trail a path made by animals in the wild.

habitat the natural environment in which plants or animals normally thrive.

javelina a collared peccary, which is a medium-sized hoofed mammal with sharp teeth that looks like a wild boar but isn't one.

lagomorphs plant-eating mammals including hares, rabbits, and pikas.

neutral zone a buffer zone between two sides that normally may not interact peacefully.

obligate carnivore an animal that survives on a strict diet of meat.

opportunistic hunter an animal that hunts whatever prey is available.

parley to hold peace talks.

pelage the fur of a mammal.

predator an animal that lives by preying on other animals.

prey an animal that is hunted by another animal for food.

quarry an animal that is hunted by a predator; prey.

raptor a bird of prey, such as an owl or hawk.

rodent a small furry gnawing animal, such as a mouse, rat, squirrel, or beaver, whose teeth never stop growing.

scavenge to search or hunt for discarded food or dead animals.

solitary living alone without others.

suburb a residential area near or outside of a city.

urban area a city.

About the author:

DIANE R. HANOVER, a writer who grew up in the Catalina foothills and lives outside of Tucson, Arizona, treasures her own encounters with local bobcats and all desert wildlife.

About the illustrator:

LOU LEWIS (1915-2014) began painting in oils in 1999, working from his studio in the Catalina foothills of Tucson, Arizona. He particularly loved painting the bobcats that came to his backyard.

For information on using *A Little Book of Bobcats* in classrooms, as well as downloadable worksheets, visit www.picturerockspublishing.com.

www.ingramcontent.com/pod-product-compliance
Lightning Source LLC
Chambersburg PA
CBHW042009090426

42811CB00015B/1596